Bhairava Chalisa

Published in Sanskriti Press
by Rupa Publications India Pvt. Ltd 2025
7/16, Ansari Road, Daryaganj
New Delhi 110002

Sales centres:
Bengaluru Chennai
Hyderabad Jaipur Kathmandu
Kolkata Mumbai Prayagraj

Edition copyright © Rupa Publications India Pvt. Ltd 2025

All rights reserved.
No part of this publication may be reproduced, transmitted,
or stored in a retrieval system, in any form or by any means,
electronic, mechanical, photocopying, recording or otherwise,
without the prior permission of the publisher.

P-ISBN: 978-93-7003-038-1
E-ISBN: 978-93-7003-550-8

First impression 2025

10 9 8 7 6 5 4 3 2 1

Printed in India

This book is sold subject to the condition that it shall not, by way of
trade or otherwise, be lent, resold, hired out, or otherwise circulated,
without the publisher's prior consent, in any form of binding or cover
other than that in which it is published.

Contents

Introduction / 5

Chalisa / 9

काल भैरव जी की आरती / 88

Kaal Bhairav Ji Ki Aarti / 91

Introduction

The Bhairava Chalisa, a powerful and profound hymn dedicated to Lord Bhairava, resonates with the raw energy and fierce protection that define this fearsome form of Shiva. Revered as the guardian of time, space, and the spiritual realm, Bhairava is both a destroyer of evil and a protector of the righteous. With each verse of the Chalisa, devotees invoke his intense presence, seeking his blessings to remove obstacles, protect from harm, and purify the soul. This ancient prayer, rich in devotion, offers not only reverence but also a call for strength and transformation through Bhairava's divine power.

It is undeniable that the Bhairava Chalisa has a unique potency, one that draws those who seek divine intervention with utmost sincerity. The hymns encapsulate Bhairava's fierce and dynamic nature, capturing the essence of destruction that clears the path for new beginnings. Chanting the Chalisa brings a sense of empowerment, as if calling upon Bhairava's forceful yet protective energy to dismantle negativity and restore balance. Through the words, devotees find courage to face challenges head-on and to conquer the darkness in their lives.

But what makes the Bhairava Chalisa so compelling? For many, it is not just the fierceness of Bhairava, but the profound symbolism of his role in Hindu mythology.

As a manifestation of Shiva, Bhairava embodies the paradox of destruction and creation, the constant cycle of life, death, and rebirth. Each verse of the Chalisa speaks to this duality, invoking Bhairava's presence to dispel fear and bring clarity. His power is not simply about annihilation, but also about purification, enlightenment, and the ultimate liberation of the soul from worldly attachments.

With each chant, there is an undeniable sense of being in the presence of a divine force that is both overwhelming and comforting. His protection is fierce, yet filled with love for his devotees, and the power within these verses is enough to transform any lingering doubts into unwavering faith.

The Bhairava Chalisa, therefore, is not just a prayer of fear or power—it is a prayer of transformation. It invites the devotee to witness and harness the divine force of

Bhairava, to confront the shadows in one's life, and to rise above them, purified and strengthened. Through the recitation of these verses, devotees seek more than protection—they seek a deeper understanding of the cosmic balance between creation and destruction, and the courage to face life's most challenging trials with unwavering faith.

Chalisa

दोहा

श्री गणपति गुरु गौरी पद, प्रेम सहित धरि माथ ।
चालीसा वंदन करो, श्री शिव भैरवनाथ ॥

Shri Ganapati Guru Gauri Pad,
Prem Sahit Dhari Maath.
Chalisa Vandana Karo,
Shri Shiv Bhairavanath.

With love, I place at the feet of Lord
Ganapati, Guru, and Gauri,
I bow to Lord Shiva Bhairavanath and
offer this Chalisa.

श्री भैरव संकट हरण, मंगल करण कृपाल ।
श्याम वरण विकराल वपु, लोचन लाल विशाल

Shri Bhairav Sankat Harn,
Mangal Karan Kripal.
Shyam Varna Vikraal Vapu,
Lochan Laal Vishal.

Lord Bhairav removes all obstacles, and is the merciful bestower of good fortune. His dark complexion and terrifying form, with large, red, and vast eyes.

जय जय श्री काली के लाला ।
जयति जयति काशी-कुतवाला ॥

Jai Jai Shri Kaali Ke Laala.
Jayati Jayati Kashi-Kutwala.

Hail to Lord Kali's son, Hail to the protector of Kashi (Varanasi).

जयति बटुक-भैरव भय हारी ।
जयति काल-भैरव बलकारी ॥

Jayati Batuk-Bhairav Bhay Haari.
Jayati Kaal-Bhairav Balkari.

Hail to Batuk-Bhairav, the destroyer of fear,
Hail to Kaal-Bhairav, the one of immense power.

जयति नाथ-भैरव विख्याता ।
जयति सर्व-भैरव सुखदाता ।।

Jayati Nath-Bhairav Vikhyata.
Jayati Sarv-Bhairav Sukhdata.

Hail to Lord Bhairav, renowned in all directions,
Hail to the Lord of all Bhairavs, the giver of joy.

भैरव रूप कियो शिव धारण ।
भव के भार उतारण कारण ।।

Bhairav Roop Kiyo Shiv Dhaaran.
Bhav Ke Bhaar Utaran Karan.

Bhairav assumed the form of Shiva,
To relieve the burden of worldly existence.

भैरव रव सुनि हवै भय दूरी ।
सब विधि होय कामना पूरी ॥

Bhairav Rav Suni Havai Bhay Doori.
Sab Vidhi Hoy Kamna Pooree.

The sound of Bhairav's roar removes all fear,
And all desires are fulfilled in every way.

शेष महेश आदि गुण गायो ।
काशी-कोतवाल कहलायो ।।

Shesh Mahesh Aadi Gun Gaayo.
Kashi-Kotwal Kehlayo.

Shesh and Mahesh sing praises of the
divine qualities,
He is called the protector of Kashi.

जटा जूट शिर चंद्र विराजत ।
बाला मुकुट बिजायठ साजत ॥

Jata Joot Shir Chandra Virajat.
Bala Mukut Bijayath Sajat.

His matted hair holds the moon on his head,
And the crown of youth adorns him beautifully.

कटि करधनी घुंघरू बाजत ।
दर्शन करत सकल भय भाजत ॥

Kati Kardhani Ghungroo Baajat.
Darshan Kart Sakal Bhay Bhaajat.

His waist is adorned with a bell,
And anyone who gazes upon him is freed
from fear.

जीवन दान दास को दीन्ह्यो ।
कीन्ह्यो कृपा नाथ तब चीन्ह्यो ॥

Jeevan Daan Daas Ko Deenyo.
Keenhyo Kripa Nath Tab Cheenyo.

He gave the gift of life to his devotee,
And showed his grace upon him.

वसि रसना बनि सारद-काली ।
दीन्ह्यो वर राख्यो मम लाली ॥

Vasi Rasna Bani Sarad-Kali.
Deenyo Var Rakhyo Mam Lali.

His tongue became like the Saraswati and Kali,
And he granted blessings, keeping me safe and beloved.

धन्य धन्य भैरव भय भंजन ।
जय मनरंजन खल दल भंजन ॥

Dhanya Dhanya Bhairav Bhay Bhanjan.
Jai Manaranjan Khal Dal Bhanjan.

Blessed is Bhairav, the remover of fear,
Hail to the one who destroys the enemies
and brings joy.

कर त्रिशूल डमरू शुचि कोड़ा ।
कृपा कटाक्ष सुयश नहिं थोड़ा ॥

Kar Trishul Damru Shuchi Koda.
Kripa Kataksha Suyash Nahin Thoda.

With his trident, damru, and pure rod,
His gracious glance bestows immense fame.

जो भैरव निर्भय गुण गावत ।
अष्टसिद्धि नव निधि फल पावत ॥

Jo Bhairav Nirbhay Gun Gavat.
Ashtasiddhi Nav Nidhi Phal Pavat.

Whoever sings the fearless virtues of Bhairav,
Will gain the eight siddhis and nine treasures.

रूप विशाल कठिन दुख मोचन ।
क्रोध कराल लाल दुहुं लोचन ॥

Roop Vishal Kathin Dukh Mochan.
Krodh Karaal Laal Duhun Lochan.

His form is vast and he is the remover of great sufferings,
His eyes are red with anger, terrifying to behold.

अगणित भूत प्रेत संग डोलत ।
बम बम बम शिव बम बम बोलत ॥

Aganit Bhoot Pret Sang Dolat.
Bam Bam Bam Shiv Bam Bam Bolat.

He is surrounded by countless ghosts and spirits,
They chant 'Bam Bam Bam' and call upon Shiva.

रुद्रकाय काली के लाला ।
महा कालहू के हो काला ॥

Rudrakaya Kaali Ke Laala.
Maha Kaalahu Ke Ho Kaala.

He is the Rudra form, the son of Kali,
And he himself is the dark one of great time (Mahakaal).

बटुक नाथ हो काल गंभीरा ।
श्वेत रक्त अरु श्याम शरीरा ॥

Batuk Nath Ho Kaal Gambheera.
Shvet Rakt Aru Shyam Shareera.

He is Batuk, the lord of time, with a serious form,
His body is white, red, and dark in color.

करत नीनहूं रूप प्रकाशा ।
भरत सुभक्तन कहं शुभ आशा ॥

Karat Neenahoon Roop Prakasha.
Bharat Subhaktan Kahan Shubh Asha.

His form is radiant even in deep sleep,
The devotees of Bharat (India) have
hopeful aspirations.

रत्न जड़ित कंचन सिंहासन ।
व्याघ्र चर्म शुचि नर्म सुआनन ॥

Ratna Jadhit Kanchan Singhasan.
Vyaghra Charma Shuchi Narm Suanan.

He sits on a golden throne adorned with jewels,
Wearing the skin of a tiger, his face is both pure and soft.

तुमहि जाइ काशिहिं जन ध्यावहिं ।
विश्वनाथ कहं दर्शन पावहिं ॥

Tumhi Jai Kashihem Jan Dhyavahin.
Vishwanath Kahan Darshan Paavahin.

Whoever meditates upon you, Kashi's protector,
Will see the divine form of Lord Vishwanath (Shiva).

जय प्रभु संहारक सुनन्द जय ।
जय उन्नत हर उमा नन्द जय ॥

Jai Prabhu Sanharak Sunand Jai.
Jai Unnat Har Uma Nand Jai.

Hail to the Lord of destruction, the giver of joy,
Hail to the exalted Lord, the son of Uma (Parvati).

भीम त्रिलोचन स्वान साथ जय ।
वैजनाथ श्री जगतनाथ जय ॥

Bheem Trilochan Swaan Saath Jai.
Vaijnath Shri Jagatnath Jai.

Hail to the mighty, the three-eyed one,
with the dog companion,
Hail to Vaijnath, the Lord of the universe.

महा भीम भीषण शरीर जय ।
रुद्र त्रयम्बक धीर वीर जय ॥

Maha Bhim Bhishan Shareer Jai.
Rudra Trayambak Dheer Veer Jai.

Hail to the powerful one, with a terrifying form,
Hail to Rudra, the three-eyed, brave, and heroic one.

अश्वनाथ जय प्रेतनाथ जय ।
स्वानारुढ़ सयचंद्र नाथ जय ॥

Ashvanath Jai Pretanath Jai.
Swanarudh Sayachandra Nath Jai.

Hail to Ashvanath, the Lord of the horse,
Hail to the Lord of the dog, riding on the moon.

निमिष दिगंबर चक्रनाथ जय ।
गहत अनाथन नाथ हाथ जय ॥

Nimish Digambar Chakranath Jai.
Gahat Anathan Nath Haath Jai.

Hail to the one who is unclad and holds
the wheel of time,
Hail to the Lord who lifts up the helpless.

त्रेशलेश भूतेश चंद्र जय ।
क्रोध वत्स अमरेश नन्द जय ॥

Treshalesh Bhutesh Chandr Jai.
Krodh Vats Amresh Nand Jai.

Hail to the one with the crescent moon,
the Lord of spirits,
Hail to the one who nurtures anger and is
the immortal son.

श्री वामन नकुलेश चण्ड जय ।
कृत्याऊ कीरति प्रचण्ड जय ॥

Shri Vaman Nakulesh Chand Jai.
Krityayu Kirati Prachand Jai.

Hail to Lord Vaman, the master of Nakul,
Hail to the one who is the cause of great fame.

रुद्र बटुक क्रोधेश कालधर ।
चक्र तुण्ड दश पाणिव्याल धर ॥

Rudra Batuk Krodhesh Kaldhar.
Chakra Tund Dash Pani Vyal Dhar.

Hail to Rudra, Batuk, the lord of anger
and time,
Who holds the wheel and the ten heads of
serpents.

करि मद पान शम्भु गुणगावत ।
चौंसठ योगिन संग नचावत ॥

Kari Mad Paan Shambhu Gun Gavat.
Chausath Yogin Sang Nachavat.

He drinks the wine of madness, singing
praises of Lord Shambhu,
And dances with the 64 yoginis.

करत कृपा जन पर बहु ढंगा ।
काशी कोतवाल अड़बंगा ।।

Karat Kripa Jan Par Bahu Dhangha.
Kashi Kotwal Adabanga.

He showers his grace upon the devotee in many ways,
He is the fearless protector of Kashi.

देयं काल भैरव जब सोटा ।
नसै पाप मोटा से मोटा ॥

Deyam Kaal Bhairav Jab Sota.
Nasai Paap Mota Se Mota.

When the great Bhairav strikes,
All sins, no matter how great, are erased.

जनकर निर्मल होय शरीरा ।
मिटै सकल संकट भव पीरा ॥

Janakar Nirmal Hoy Shareera.
Mitae Sakal Sankat Bhav Peera.

The body of the devotee becomes pure,
And all the obstacles and pains of worldly existence vanish.

श्री भैरव भूतों के राजा ।
बाधा हरत करत शुभ काजा ॥

Shri Bhairav Bhuton Ke Raja.
Badha Harat Karat Shubh Kaja.

Lord Bhairav is the king of all beings,
He removes obstacles and performs
auspicious deeds.

ऐलादी के दुख निवारयो ।
सदा कृपाकरि काज सम्हारयो ॥

Ailadi Ke Dukh Nivaryao.
Sada Kripakari Kaaj Samharayo.

He removes the sorrows of the poor,
Always performing his duties with grace
and care.

सुन्दर दास सहित अनुरागा ।
श्री दुर्वासा निकट प्रयागा ॥

Sundar Das Sahit Anuraga.
Shri Durvasa Nikat Prayaga.

Along with his devotee, Sundar, he is filled with love,
And he is near Prayag, where the sage Durvasa resides.

श्री भैरव जी की जय लेख्यो ।
सकल कामना पूरण देख्यो ॥

Shri Bhairav Ji Ki Jai Lekhyo.
Sakal Kamana Poorn Dekhyo.

Hail to Lord Bhairav!
I have witnessed all desires being fulfilled.

जय जय जय भैरव बटुक स्वामी संकट टार ।
कृपा दास पर कीजिए शंकर के अवतार ।।
जो यह चालीसा पढ़े, प्रेम सहित सत बार ।
उस घर सर्वानंद हो, वैभव बढ़े अपार ।।

*Jai Jai Jai Bhairav Batuk Swami
Sankat Taar.
Kripa Daas Par Keejiye Shankar Ke Avatar.
Jo Yah Chalisa Padhe,
Prem Sahit Sat Baar.
Us Ghar Sarvanand Ho,
Vaibhav Badhaye Apar.*

Hail to Lord Bhairav Batuk, the one who removes all obstacles!
May you shower your grace upon your devotee, the incarnation of Shankar.
Whoever recites this Chalisa with love and devotion a hundred times,
In that home, immense joy and prosperity will grow.

इति श्री भैरूजी चालीसा सम्पूर्ण

Iti Shri Bhairuji Chalisa Sampoorn

Thus ends the **Shri Bhairuji Chalisa.**

काल भैरव जी की आरती

जय भैरव देवा, प्रभु जय भैरव देवा ।
जय काली और गौर देवी कृत सेवा ॥
॥ जय भैरव देवा...॥

तुम ही पाप उद्धारक दुःख सिन्धु तारक ।
भक्तों के सुख कारक भीषण वपु धारक ॥
॥ जय भैरव देवा...॥

वाहन श्वान विराजत कर त्रिशूल धारी ।
महिमा अमित तुम्हारी जय जय भयहारी ॥
॥ जय भैरव देवा...॥

तुम बिन देवा सेवा सफल नहीं होवे ।
चौमुख दीपक दर्शन दुःख खोवे ॥
॥ जय भैरव देवा...॥

तेल चटकी दधि मिश्रित भाषावाली तेरी ।
कृपा कीजिये भैरव, करिए नहीं देरी ॥
॥ जय भैरव देवा...॥

पाँव घुँघरू बाजत अरु डमरू दम्कावत ।

बटुकनाथ बन बालक जल मन हरषावत ।
॥ जय भैरव देवा...॥

बटुकनाथ जी की आरती जो कोई नर गावे ।
कहे धरनी धर नर मनवांछित फल पावे ॥
॥ जय भैरव देवा...॥

Kaal Bhairav Ji Ki Aarti

Jai Bhairav Deva, Prabhu Jai Bhairav Deva.
Jai Kali aur Gaur Devi krit seva.
|| Jai Bhairav Deva... ||

Tumhi paap uddharak, dukh sindhu taarak.
Bhakto ke sukh kaarak, bheeshan vapu dhaarak.
|| Jai Bhairav Deva... ||

Vahan shwaan viraajat, kar trishool dhaari.
Mahima amit tumhaari, Jai Jai Bhayahari.
|| Jai Bhairav Deva... ||

Tum bin deva seva, safal nahi hove.
Chaumukh deepak darshan, dukh khove.
|| Jai Bhairav Deva... ||

Tel chatki dadhhi mishrit bhashavali teri.
Kripa kijiye Bhairav, kariye nahi deri.
|| Jai Bhairav Deva... ||

Paanv ghungroo bajat, aru damru damkavat.
Batuknath ban baalak, jal man harshaavat.
|| Jai Bhairav Deva... ||

Batuknath ji ki aarti jo koi nar gaave.
Kahe dharni dhar nar manvaanchhit fal paave.
|| Jai Bhairav Deva... ||

Kaal Bhairav Ji Ki Aarti

Hail Lord Bhairav, O Lord, hail Bhairav.
Hail the service done by Goddess
Kali and Goddess Gauri.
|| Hail Bhairav... ||

You are the savior of sins, the one who
crosses the ocean of suffering.
You are the giver of happiness to
devotees, the bearer of a terrifying form.
|| Hail Bhairav... ||

Your vehicle is a dog,
and you hold a trident.
Your glory is immeasurable,
Hail to you, the remover of fear.
|| Hail Bhairav... ||

Without you, service to the
gods is unsuccessful.
The four-faced lamp's vision
removes all sorrow.
|| Hail Bhairav... ||

Your oil-smeared hair,
mixed with yogurt, and
your language is divine.

Bestow your grace,
Bhairav, do not delay.
|| Hail Bhairav... ||

Your feet make the sound of ghungroos
and the damru drums reverberate.
You are Batuknath, the child,
bringing joy to the heart.
|| Hail Bhairav... ||

Whoever sings the aarti of Batuknath,
says the earth will fulfill all his desires.
He will receive the desired
fruit in his heart.
|| Hail Bhairav... ||